Expand Your Personal Brand

CARLA JENKINS

Expand Your Personal Brand

Copyright © 2016 by Carla Jenkins

ISBN: 978-0-9975413-0-4

Table of Contents

Prologue

In this book Carla R. Jenkins will save you time, money and the agony of trying to figure out how to "Expand Your Personal Brand" with zero dollars in your pocket. Whether financially, personally, in business, marketing or time management, we all have a brand to cultivate and expand.

Within this book, Carla provides 20 lessons learned from trial and error all the way from zero to being a 6-figure earner. Would you like a learning curve? Would you like realistic and applicable answers to solve your personal and professional branding challenges? If the answer is yes, then this book is for you and the door is about to be opened for unlimited success branding success. You can visit site at http://carlarjenkins.com

Carla Jenkins Biography

Carla Jenkins is a phenomenal expert specializing in positive change management. She helps people capitalize upon all opportunities that positive change brings. Jenkins has received her BA in International Economics from Hiram College and her MBA from Cleveland State University. She also possesses 10 years' experience in corporate America, a LinkedIn Pulse contributor and a certified project management professional. Ms. Jenkins is the host of Positive Change with Carla radio show focusing on positive change and project management.

Having earned 4 promotions in 9 years, Jenkins has experienced and handled positive change management head on. Many people only talk about change in the negative, but change can be positive. No one talks about positive change, so Jenkins learnt how to manage this change through trial and error.

Don't Wait Until Tomorrow.
Do It Today!

1

Don't Wait, Do It Now

ASK YOURSELF A question: what do you want to drop in the future? Think about it. Okay, well why wait? Do it now. Why stay miserable? Liberate yourself from the things that weigh you down because this kind of honesty saves time and money.

Time

You have a finite amount of time on this earth. Why waste it? Honesty improves time management and eliminates waste. You sharpen your focus on what you truly want. Directed, intentional focus always increases productivity. Increased productivity means increased visibility. Increased visibility could mean increased promotions. Right now is the time to strike!

Money

How much money have you wasted going in the wrong direction? I admit that I have spent a couple of thousands of dollars pursuing another certification because I thought that it would differentiate me from others. Although this additional certification would distinguish me from my competition, I've found another certification that more closely aligns me with my future goals. Yes, I've wasted money, but I've stopped digging and realized that I am going to in another direction. I am better for it.

Conclusion
Instead of waiting, why not use this time to gain momentum towards your new goal? Remember, insanity is doing the same thing but expecting a different result. Be honest with yourself now. Your future self will thank you for it.

Exercise:
List 3-5 things that you have been putting off but can do now.

_____

_____

_____

_____

_____

_____

_____

_____

_____

_____

_____

_____

2

Getting Out of Your Comfort Zone

YOUR COMFORT ZONE is very deceiving. This comfort is a false positive. Although you feel a sense of security, it is fleeting because if you don't adapt, you die. Staying in your comfort zone is like a cocoon. Yes, this is a nice place to be, yet you will never become a butterfly unless you break out of it. Remaining in your comfort zone in the present, mortgages your future growth. Although growing pains are temporary, stagnation is permanent. You and your career will die a slow death in your comfort zone because you don't progress at the same rate as everyone else. Comfort makes our skills rusty leaning to becoming obsolete. That's why getting out of your comfort zone is a must. I have overcome my fear of the unknown. You can move beyond your comfort zone too by following these tips:

It Requires Courage.
We are all creatures of habit, and we love routine. As humans, we are scared of change because it is unfamiliar. Trying new things forces us to grow. With promoting Positivity Change in general

and myself in particular, I am going to have to speak up and give interviews. I cannot hide behind an Excel spreadsheet. Change takes courage to move beyond your comfort zone but it is necessary to get to the next level.

Face Your Fears.
Although I had a Toastmaster competent communicator certificate, I was much more analytical letting the data speak for me. Now I had to speak for 20 whole minutes on a radio show. I did it and survived confidently. Facing my fears was essential towards communicating my brand. I was still living and breathing afterward. I did not die from my public speaking fear.

Know that the worst thing that can happen when you try something new is that you might fail.
I was the second of two interviewers. This order took some of the anxiety off me, however, hearing the person preceding me made me nervous. This was not her first interview but it was mine. If I did not do well, I would have to chalk it up to experience. Okay, what if I bombed my first interview? It happened to a whole bunch of newbies. Furthermore, at least the radio host was interested in me. However, I did not and managed to keep calm. Remember that fear's acronym is false evidence appearing real. Don't succumb to F.E.A.R.

Make a Plan.
Having a plan gives you sort of order and control. I wrote down my site and summarized a few articles. These things massaged my nerves enough to go on air and promote myself without any glitches. I was able to confidently answer all of the questions.

Realize that the unknown will always be there.

You can't plan for everything, so just set out with good intentions and do your best. I didn't know that the interviewer would ask me about the future of the site. I survived that question by telling her about my dreams of expanding the site and possibly doing some cross-promotions. In addition, when she mentioned that my MBA/economics background was rare, that surprised me too. I had these degrees for over 13 years. These rarities didn't register with me because these degrees were second nature. I just put one foot in front of the other and accepted no excuses. I didn't know what questions I would be asked, but by following these tips, I made it through my first interview successfully. Hey, if I survived the unknown and my first radio interview by moving out of my comfort zone so can you!

Exercise: Overcoming Your Fear

Write down one of your biggest fears. Next, get to the heart of the matter by doing the 5 whys exercise. In project management, the 5 whys exercise is a root cause analysis technique. You ask yourself why 5 times to get to the root of the problem. Below ask yourself why 5 times to get to the bottom of your fear.

My biggest fear is _____

_____

_____

1: Why_____

2: Why_____

3: Why_____

4: Why_____

5: Why_____

_____

_____

_____

_____

3

Employing the Three C's (Clarity, Consistency and Constancy) to Improve Your Personal Career Brand

NOW MORE THAN ever, it is imperative that every professional has a personal brand. You can no longer just do your job and update your resume. The average person will have in between 7-10 jobs in his lifetime. You must actively manage your career to find the next job; hence, the importance of creating and maintaining a stellar personal career brand. The three C's towards improving your personal career brand are clarity, consistency, and constancy. These three principles are necessary towards creating your best personal brand. The combination of these three guarantees that you'll attract the people and employers in your target market.

Clarity

Dictionary.com defines clarity as 'clearness or lucidity as to perception or understanding; freedom from indistinctness or ambiguity.'

It is essential that you get clear about who you are, but, more importantly, who you **ARE NOT.** Clarity provides you with an opportunity to thrive as a specialist rather than merely survive as a generalist. It is better to know what you are not because you can create clear boundaries. You don't want to transmit mixed messages, thereby, diluting your brand. Clarity communicates a clear message of what you do. For example, if you are in HR, you don't want people coming to you about sales & marketing. The next step is to identify your competitors.

Scanning the professional landscape to see what your competitors are doing, and more importantly, what they are not doing. It is critical towards how you'll position yourself to stand out. Learn from your competitors' mistakes and capitalize upon the areas that they aren't already in. Being the first mover in an unsaturated area, positions you towards becoming an expert. For instance, if you're in HR but there aren't as many people working with newly returned war veterans, then this is a niche where you can employ your transferable skills and become an expert. Once you've used clarity to identify your competitors, you can then focus on marketing your competitive advantage to the world.

Your competitive advantage is the one thing that you do better than anyone else. Having a clear definition of this advantage will attract more people and opportunities. In HR, do you compile benefits packages in a way that a new employee understands? Your ability to translate industry-specific jargon into non-technical language without diluting its content is your competitive advantage. You can convert this into a special niche and be seen as an expert. Once you're seen as an expert, more people will come to you.

Consistency

Consistency is defined as 'steadfast adherence to the same principles, course, form, etc.' In order to keep current in this increasingly global and competitive landscape, you must be consistent. This means consistently communicating the same message offline and online. Take some time to review how your professional brand comes across because it's imperative that you are consistent in both areas.

Make sure that your resume and LinkedIn profile are the same. If you've attained a new certification or a promotion, list them on both. An outdated LinkedIn profile sends an inconsistent message. For example, if you've been promoted from HR Specialist to Senior HR Specialist, you must list this change. Recruiters who might be interested in you for one job, may not know that you have a new job or certification. It would be bad for your professional reputation if a recruiter contacts you about a specific position but learns that you're in another position. Recruiters talk with other recruiters who might work at the company that interests you. You don't want this kind of mistake to precede you before applying for a job. Putting the most recent information on your LinkedIn page guarantees that recruiters can see if you are the best fit for a potential job.

Constancy

Constancy is defined as 'uniformity or regularity, as in qualities or conditions; invariableness.' Being highly visible online & offline to your target market is indispensable. There are many ways to increase your visibility to ensure that the right people see your talents. Offline opportunities include joining meet-ups, alumni chapters, and professional organizations. In addition, you can be visible through business cards and stationery. Handing out your personal business cards is an effective marketing tool that generates high visibility. Furthermore, you can send thank you letters using your own stationery. Regarding online visibility opportunities, you can register for LinkedIn professional groups, follow people on Twitter or like Facebook pages of companies which you want to work for. Moreover, you can also start a blog. Continuing with the HR example, you can write about interviewing new applicants, dispensing benefits information, handling attrition and completing retirement packages.

Creating a Communication Plan to Incorporate the Three C's
Creating a communications plan is a great way to merge the offline and online visibility tools to achieve clarity, consistency and constancy. Your plan manages how, what, why, when, and where to deploy your offline and online strategies. For instance, you decide to post weekly HR-related articles in your LinkedIn feed. This action achieves clarity (HR), consistency (on message) and constancy (weekly). Your communication plans ensure that you regularly do something constructive towards promoting your personal career brand. Incorporating three C's of clarity, consistency and constancy guarantees increased demand for your personal career brand.

Exercise: Brand Clarity

It is time to get clear on your personal brand. Use this space below to write down these three things:

- What you are good at

_____

_____

- What you are not good at

_____

_____

- Take 1-2 items from the 'what you are good at' list and write down how you will promote each one in the marketplace

_____

_____

_____

_____

_____

_____

4

Handling High-Visibility Projects as a Newbie

OFTENTIMES, WHEN EMPLOYEES are handed their first highly visible project, they panic. They are new and don't have a roadmap. I want you to continue getting more projects. More projects equal more visibility. This visibility can translate into more promotions. Following these four tips will help any newbie.

Be thankful that someone had entrusted you with this opportunity.
This is a positive. Instead of being overwhelmed, be happy to view this as a chance to prove yourself in the marketplace increasing your professional credibility and visibility. Taking this more optimistic viewpoint enables you to devise an approach upon this new assignment.

Conduct project and personnel research.
First, review the project materials. You have to know what you are undertaking. Possessing familiarity with your project lets you

excel. Next, research the people on your project team. You can view their bios on the company Intranet or their LinkedIn profiles. It is essential to know your future team members' personalities and work histories. This information lets you effectively create a staffing management plan to execute the project.

Create your own personal project schedule.
Creating your own personal project schedule helps you envision it. You can also incorporate a what-if analysis covering any and every possibility because projects don't always go as planned.

Practice presenting your plan.
Although you've never done it before, you are still the project leader and must exude confidence to your workers and management. Prepare in the mirror before work to get rid of the jitters. Having these ready-made answers from your personal project schedule are necessary because management wants a definitive response regardless of how the people act and the project is going.

Exercise: Project Management Strategy

Chron.com defines project management strategy as 'the primary goal of gaining the competitive advantage by focusing on the organization's overall direction.' In this exercise, document how you are going to capitalize upon your competitive advantage by defining your own project management strategy.

_____

_____

_____

_____

_____

_____

_____

_____

_____

5

How to Stop Paralysis
of Analysis

PARALYSIS OF ANALYSIS happens to everyone. We think about things too much and all of a sudden, they snowball and overwhelm us. Your original thought, which was derived from good intentions, now becomes unmanageable. We've all been there. Here are my 3 tips for breaking free:

Break the big goal into many smaller parts.
Paralysis of analysis is usually due to thinking too much about everything. To combat this arresting of thought, you must go from the general to the specific. This requires using a filter to whittle down the number of ideas swirling around in your head. Instead of doing 5 things at once, do 1 thing 5 separate times. Once you centralize your focus on one specific part, the paralysis stops and you can restart again.

Pick one small part and start working on it.
Working on one small part lets you generate small wins. These small victories bolster your confidence and build your momentum. Using the 5 parts as an example, if you complete 1 of the 5 parts

that equals 20% progress. Each completion puts you closer towards your 100% goal.

Celebrate the small wins to sustain momentum.
Once you're done, take time out to celebrate your win. Focus on the present and not the future. Rather than loathing that you aren't at 100% yet, acknowledge that the 20% that you've completed has put you closer towards your goal.

Implementing these three tips propel you further along towards accomplishing your overall goal and demolishing paralysis of analysis.

Exercise: Get out of your own head
Write down everything in your head to free yourself.

_____

_____

_____

_____

_____

_____

_____

_____

_____

_____

_____

_____

6

Self-Investment is the Best Investment

THE GLOBAL WORKPLACE is uncertain. You don't know if you'll be with your current employer by the end of this week. Even the federal government isn't safe from layoffs with sequestration. Self-investment is certain, but the question everyone poses is; how do you afford self-investment on a shoestring budget? Here are some resources that I have found to help you achieve self-investment at a cheaper rate.

Regardless of what happens, start saving 5%-10% of your monthly income.
It provides you with a cushion to afford options. I've used this cushion to self-finance my PMP certification and community college courses advancing my career.

Look at your employer's resources.
Your company might offer training programs, tuition assistance for college courses and leadership development programs. These corporate courses let you cultivate and develop the necessary skills

to get to the next level. I have been selected into two leadership development programs with two separate federal agencies. I have acquired new skills and obtained new sponsors who would advocate for me internally.

Community colleges
They have residency discounts with people in the county. Community colleges also specialize in workforce retraining, so you won't feel out of place with younger students like at four-year colleges. Community colleges have perennially catered to the needs of older workers retooling themselves for the current marketplace.

Libraries
Don't sleep on libraries. They offer the best career resources. Many libraries provide free computer courses and databases to upgrade your skill set. Furthermore, they also have career books and magazines that you can read to refine yourself.

Professional organizations
Professional organizations offer continuing education through their chapters. Furthermore, they provide discounts on industry certifications. In addition, these organizations also have continuing education seminars and workshops to inform their members on current industry trends.

Alumni Associations
Many college alumni associations have online and offline educational discounts for their members. You can also use their networks to ask other members for career resources and company introductions.

MOOCs (Coursera and MIT OpenCourseware)

Massive Open Online Courses (MOOCs) offer free resources to upgrade your skills set on your own time. MIT OpenCourseware possesses a wealth of free courses. Coursera offers free courses and certificates for $49. Some of these courses might qualify personal development units to renew your professional certification.

Online Courses (Ed2Go)

Ed2Go is an affordable online course website that many community colleges collaborate with to offer their students more options. Depending on the college, classes range from $99-$130 apiece. I have used Ed2Go to take and renew my project management certification.

Hopefully, any of these free or low-cost options will enable you to jumpstart your self-investment journey. Self-investment is the best investment.

Exercise: Research the educational resources on this list finding costs and start dates

_____

_____

_____

_____

_____

_____

_____

_____

_____

_____

_____

_____

Course	Start Date	Cost

7

Three Steps for Planning
for Interruptions

L IFE HAPPENS. INTERRUPTIONS occur and we
must deal with them while still delivering our work on
time, on topic and under budget! Even though we want
to always experience positive change, negative things happen. We
must adequately prepare ourselves because the work still must get
done! Here are my top three things to complete your work even
with interruptions.

Add some cushion
Don't schedule so tight. There will always be some interruptions.
I allocate 10% buffer just in case of emergencies. You need a time
cushion just in case you have to be the backup representative at
a meeting you're not even supposed to be in because your other
colleague is unavailable. Time cushions enable you enough lead
time to get back on track and complete your work.

Develop contingency plans

A contingency plan is a backup plan. You need at least one contingency plan in place just in case your original plan doesn't go accordingly. There are always changes in budgets, priorities, and time so you have to adjust to ensure that the work still gets done. For instance, your operating budget is $1 million but due to the recession, it has been cut to $500,000. Your contingency plan should have been developed just in case one of the triple constraints (scope, cost and time) is cut. Your project scope will have to be cut too. No one cares that the budget is cut. They still want the work done.

I recommend having more than one contingency plan. I have experienced too much change and turbulence in the workplace that I have been forced to create multiple contingency plans. Therefore, have not only plan B but C, D and E if necessary!

Learn to reprioritize

Sometimes after interruptions, your work priorities shift. Some things are more important than others. When there are quarterly or end-of-the-year deadlines, time—sensitive projects are higher priorities. Quarterly time-sensitive matters and urgent deadlines are interruptions because they only occur every three to four times a year. If your other work shares the same deadline as the high-priority work, management may let you delay submitting it until after the quarter.

Adding cushion, developing contingency plans and learning to reprioritize enable you to bounce back from workplace interruptions and finish your work on time.

Exercise: Write a contingency plan.

It is the end of the second quarter and you have your upcoming quarterly progress review meeting with your boss. You also have a major project that is due. Write down your contingency plan. Include time cushions to ensure that the work gets done.

_____

_____

_____

_____

_____

_____

_____

_____

_____

_____

_____

8

Five Differences Between Busy and Productive People

TODAY PEOPLE ARE running around busier than ever. They are on their phones, laptops, tablets and desktops. However, they are tired and less productive. People falsely mistake busyness for productivity because they doing so many things. Productive means finishing the tasks that you start. Here are 5 differences between busy and productive people.

Productive people don't care if people are looking. Busy people do things to put on airs.
Productive people announce outcomes when things are actually done. Busy people tell you the play-by-play. The problem is that many things can go wrong. What happens if something doesn't go according to plan or doesn't come to fruition? Busy people think that constantly announcing whatever they are doing is keeping people informed but in reality it is oversharing. People don't care the number of steps involved. They just care about the outcome.

Productive people only put three items on their to-do list.
Keeping shorter to-do lists don't overwhelm you. One to three things are manageable. Having 10 things on your to-do list shocks your brain.

Productive people single-task. Busy people multitask.
Multitasking is a lie! It makes you tired because you are expending so much energy doing ten things at a time. Furthermore, it overloads your brain. If you are allocating the same amount of time towards 10 things, then you are doing 1/10. There is a very big difference between 10/1 versus 1/10. Do one thing, ten times versus ten things, one time. When you do one thing ten times, you complete ten things. However, if you do ten things one time, none of these ten things are completed.

Productive people say yes strategically. Busy people say yes to everything.
Let's define strategic versus tactic. Strategic means long-term. Tactic means short-term. Productive people are strategic. Busy people are tactical. When productive people say yes, they're thinking of the long-term implications of their decisions. Busy people only think about the right now. That's tactical because it's short-term.

Busy people are distracted. Productive people are focused.
Productive people don't get sidetracked because their best friends are calling them on their jobs. They tell their friends that they cannot call them at work because they are focused on completing their tasks. Busy people take their friends' phone calls during their breaks that spill over into work time because everything is important.

These 5 busy versus productive people distinctions will help you improve my time management and reduce being overwhelmed by focusing on what really matters.

Exercise:

Pair down your to-do list. Take out your current to-do list. Are there any activities that you can merge into one task or drop altogether? The goal is to have a to-do list with a maximum of three things on it.

_____

_____

_____

_____

_____

_____

_____

_____

_____

_____

_____

9

Keeping the Momentum Going Until You Win

OFTENTIMES, PEOPLE STOP working as hard once the momentum starts accelerating. You gain some traction and you think that the 'machine can runs itself.' That's the biggest mistake you can ever make because this is exactly the time when you should be working in overdrive. You want to continue the good fortune that you're currently experiencing. Below I offer the why and the how to keep the momentum going.

Why keep the momentum going?
You're not done yet. You don't celebrate wins when you're only 60%-70% there. You haven't achieved anything yet.

Remember how hard it was to get started
Paradigm shifts consume time and energy. You are changing your mind and routine. Imagine if you stop in the middle. You have just sent a signal to your brain to revert back to your old routine. You'll have to summon up the same amount of strength and fortitude to

restart. Keep going because you won't have the same enthusiasm doing it over again.

Don't look like a quitter

Stopping in the middle makes you look like a quitter. Who wants to be one? People avoid quitters like the plague. Quitting makes you look uncommitted.

How to keep the momentum going

Remember that once you're done, you don't have to do it ever again. For example, part of the joy of completing your degree is knowing that you're done. Yes, trade war stories at the alumni gala but you're glad the 'battle of earning your degree' is over.

Remember why you've started

There will always be days when you aren't as enthusiastic. These are the days when you remember your why. Your why is the ultimate reason why you are deciding to change. Whether it's a better life, health or more money, we all have a 'why' for wanting change. You want to have a better future. You've made a decision to change your current circumstances because you don't want to live your old life anymore. Following through until the end is an important reason to keep the momentum going.

Insanity is doing the same thing but expecting a different result.

You don't want to be in the same place as you've started. Don't get stuck in the mud. Remember how immobilizing mediocrity was until you started doing something differently. By keeping the momentum going, you are accomplishing two things simultaneously:

distancing yourself from your old self and getting closer to who you want to become. Decide to stay unstuck by keeping the momentum going right now. Your future self will thank you for it.

Exercise: List your top 5 distractions

1: _____

2: _____

3: _____

4: _____

5: _____

10

Meeting Deadlines Through Prioritization

W ITH COMPETITIVE PRIORITIES and over-lapping deadlines, the workplace (and the world for that matter) can be a juggling act. You are forced to prioritize by obligations in the order of importance. Usually this is easy, but sometimes two or more things have equal importance or the same deadlines.

Here are my 4 steps towards prioritizing without being stressed out.

Prioritize what needs to be completed.
Some things are more important than others. These high-priority tasks require more time and effort. Fast-tracking is a technique used for these essential projects. Activities that were once done in order are now done together. Doing tasks simultaneously reduces the amount of time necessary to complete the entire project.

Break your projects down into smaller pieces.
If it's a big task that will take the whole month or quarter, break each piece of the project down by weeks. If it is a small task requiring a

couple of weeks, plan each piece by day. Daily and weekly planning achieve two things: they don't overwhelm you and they let you track your progress. The goal is not to get overwhelmed by the enormity of your objective. Breaking down your tasks accomplish this.

Monitor your plans.
It is essential to monitor everything that you do because hiccups will occur. When they do happen, you will be able to identify them with your contingency plan. Contingency plans are mandatory because things rarely go according to plan.

Reward yourself at the end of each completed phase.
Stopping to catch your breath is very important during this time. You don't want to get so ingrained in your plan that you don't acknowledge your progress. Each completed phase puts you one-step closer towards completing your small and big tasks. I hope that these 4 steps will help you organize your work so that you can save time, money and, most importantly, sanity.

Exercise: Monitor Your Plan

When the original plan is not working, people automatically ditch it and go to Plan B. That would be premature because you do not have any measurements to evaluate performance. It is essential to know what is wrong with your original plan and how you can fix it before going onto plan B. You need to have some metrics that will let you know when your original plan is not working. This exercise will help you develop the metrics necessary to measure performance.

Example: You are in change of an air conditioning system. The machine is supposed to stay at 65 degrees. If it registers 67 degrees or higher seven times, then pull it from operations and fix it. If after reinstalling the machine, it still malfunctions then you pull it and go with another air conditioning machine. This second machine is your plan B.

Now it is your turn. Take any company metric you use to measure success, and write down a monitoring plan.

What is your metric:

_____

What is the number or percentage that would force a review:

_____

What situation would happen for you to go with plan B:

_____

_____

11

Avoiding Scope Creep

A S PROJECT MANAGERS, scope creep is one of the biggest nuisances to bear. You usually don't see it coming until it too late. There is a small workaround request that doesn't cost any money so it gets approved; and, all of a sudden, there are more requests for additional features, some of which are not even in the contract. Now that tiny crack becomes a dam and your project is drowning in cost overruns, low morale and lack of direction. We can avoid scope creep by employing these five steps:

1. **Stay vigilant throughout the entire project**
    You are the project manager. The buck stops with you. You are in charge of the project management plan; and, hence, the scope. It is your job to protect the integrity of the scope baseline.

2. **Define project scope**
    Once you define the scope, stick to it. The scope is what is covered by the contract. Deviating from it could mean a lawsuit and claims administration. Steer clear of any legal action by adhering to the project scope statement.

3. **Manage stakeholder engagement**

   Stakeholder request is often the source of most scope creep. That is why is it critical to manage stakeholders effectively. The Project Management Body of Knowledge (PMBOK) defines the manage stakeholder engagement process as 'communicating and working with stakeholders to meet their needs/expectations, address issues as they occur and foster the appropriate stakeholder engagement in project activities throughout the project life cycle.'

   Often times the stakeholder with the most project money is the one throwing all of his weight around pushing unauthorized change requests. Here is where you politely remind him that he will get all of the blame when it goes wrong, there is a change management plan and that he can submit his change before the board for approval. You have to take the hard line with stakeholders because once someone gets an unauthorized change, then everyone else floods your inbox with theirs.

4. **Uphold the change control process**

   The change control process is documented in the project management plan. Uphold it at all costs. You should immediately defer all change requests to the change control board. Following this protocol eliminates scope creep as well as stopping gold plating in its tracks. Upholding the change control process has another benefit: people view it as objective because the process is documented in the project management plan.

5. **Leverage technology**

   Technology is your friend. You should leverage every approved software, mobile app and file sharing system to your advantage.

Using software to trace requirements, and measure project execution, time, cost and scope are surefire ways to avoid scope creep.

Following these five steps will help you avoid scope creep on all projects big and small.

Exercise: Crashing a Project

The Project Management Body of Knowledge (PMBOK) defines crashing as 'a technique used to shorten the schedule duration for the least incremental cost by adding resources.' Crashing increases your budget but decreases your timeline. If you're in a crunch, you may have to resort to this. With crashing, your risk increases for two reasons: 1) you are accelerating your project and 2) you are on your project's critical path. The critical path is the scheduling timeline where there is no extra time. If something goes wrong, it derails the entire project. Crashing puts all of my work on the critical path so there is no room for error. This second reason is why crashing can be so dangerous.

_____

_____

_____

_____

_____

_____

_____

_____

_____

12

Assess, Action, and Adapt

PEOPLE ARE ALWAYS looking into the future relegating their present to wishful thinking. That would be a grave error because there are many things that you can do today to make your personal and work lives better. Use today as your springboard into soaring higher in the future.

Here are my three A's (Assess, Action and Adapt) for using time to your full advantage.

Assess

You have to be brutally honest with yourself and your progress or lack thereof. Conduct a full autopsy of this year by doing a full strengths, weaknesses, opportunities and threats (SWOT) analysis. Examine your strengths, weaknesses, opportunities and threats. Ask yourself; what has gone right? These are your strengths and opportunities. Then ask yourself what has gone wrong? These are your weaknesses and threats.

Action

Now that you've written down your SWOT analysis, you will devote this time towards developing longer term plans based on this analysis. You can drill this plan down into quarters, months or weeks if necessary. Then, you want to take your strengths and opportunities and maximize these for the New Year. Exploit them to the fullest. See how you can magnify your strengths at work and home towards making your life easier. Conversely, you want to minimize your weaknesses and threats. The action plan's goal is to eliminate what you have done wrong so that you can do more of what's going right. This annual action plan serves as your baseline for future progress.

Adapt

Most people think that once you write the plan, it is written in stone and can never be changed. That cannot be any further from the truth! It is okay and actually encouraged to change your plan after you've created it because situations change. Your original plan is your baseline. The purpose of your annual plan is to guide you throughout the year. When things change, you have to adapt.

Don't waste another year of winging it by hoping that everything goes well for you on the whimsical New Year's resolutions that you've made at midnight. Make your year (and life) easier by incorporating the three A's (Assess, Action and Adapt).

Exercise: How to Create a SWOT Analysis

Write down your strengths, weaknesses, opportunities and threats.

Strengths	Weaknesses
1.	1.
2.	2.
3.	3.
4.	4.
5.	5.
Opportunities	**Threats**
1.	1.
2.	2.
3.	3.
4.	4.
5.	5.

13

Promote Your Competitive Advantage

DEVELOPING AND PROMOTING your competitive advantage are indispensable towards getting the best job out there. Before I go any further, let me define what competitive advantage is. The definition for competitive advantage is 'a condition or circumstance that puts a company in a favorable or superior business position'. Individuals have competitive advantages just like companies.

How to develop your competitive advantage
Doing a SWOT analysis is a way towards finding your competitive advantage. SWOT stands for strengths, weaknesses, opportunities and threats. Strengths and weaknesses are internal. Opportunities and threats are external. Use exercise 12 to create a SWOT analysis. From the SWOT analysis, you will now know what you are good at doing. Once you know this, the next step is promoting your competitive advantage in the marketplace.

How to promote your competitive advantage

There are three steps towards effectively promoting your competitive advantage. These steps are: research your industry, leverage your transferable skills and avoid myopia. When you research your industry, look at what your competitors are doing. What are the trends that are out there? What pieces of the current trends can you incorporate in your repertoire to increase your marketability? If you can find an angle to exploit, then go for it because this is your competitive advantage.

The next step is to leverage your transferable skills. You have discovered them from doing the SWOT analysis. These are your strengths. Look to see if some of your transferable skills overlap with the current industry trends. In addition, see if these skills can work in other industries, which leads me to the third and final step: don't be myopic. You can work in more than one field. You can also have more than one competitive advantage. You don't exclusively only have to have either hard skill or soft skill competitive advantages. In this global marketplace, you will need multiple competitive advantages in order to be hired.

By following these steps, you will increase your competitive advantage marketing capability.

Exercise: Finding your competitive advantage and applying it to the marketplace.

Write down what skills you are good at.

- Research LinkedIn advanced search feature to see if there are jobs in your area.
- Look at the job description.
  - Look at the verbs and the phrases
  - Look for the job skill
- Taylor your resume using the same words.

_____

_____

_____

_____

_____

_____

_____

_____

_____

14

What You Need to Leave Behind

WHEN WE BECOME successful, things, people and places change. You are not stationary. Your life has become dynamic. Sometimes these changes means that certain people and behaviors must be left behind in order to continue experiencing more success. Certain people can be emotional vampires sucking the life out of your dreams. They need to be dropped like a bad habit; and, you must do it now. You cannot sabotage yourself.

Negative mindset and people
Resolve to let these people go! Why are you letting people steal your joy? Don't bring this baggage with you. Dropping these ne'er do wells liberates you to take more time for yourself. You cannot bring the would've, should've and could've with you.

You must also erase the negative mindset. It takes time to distance yourself from negativity. You cannot just flip a switch on and poof be gone! You need to shift your mindset from doubt to doing. It takes time to move past it; but eradicating negativity is something that you need to leave behind.

Physical and mental clutter

Stress wears you down. Your body and immune system break down. Remove yourself from stressful situations. If your work environment stresses you out, then hire a resume writer to revise yours.

Mental clutter obstructs your thought process. Removing the mental clutter gives your brain new space to think new thoughts. Buy a composition notebook and write down all of your thoughts. No matter how random, jot them down. This is called the brain dump. You are dumping all of your thoughts on a piece of paper that gives your brain more space to generate new ones. Mental clutter slows you down from having better thoughts. Better thoughts = better life.

Incomplete tasks

You cannot go into the future leaving things undone. It is essential that you complete as many tasks as possible. Finishing them liberates your time for other things. Completing it frees up your time to do something else. You will see a very big change in energy when you finish something because you won't have to do it again. Leaving these three things behind guarantees a more productive life.

Exercise: Silencing your inner critic
What are the top 3 negative things you say about yourself? Go to
a thesaurus. Replace those with positive words.

_____

_____

_____

_____

_____

_____

_____

_____

_____

_____

_____

_____

15

5 Tips for Maximizing Your Conference Experience

ATTENDING INDUSTRY CONFERENCES are necessary towards promoting your personal brand. You cannot do all of your networking behind the screen on LinkedIn. Relationships are still people first. It would be nice to know the person behind the avatar. You will need more than just business cards in order to make your mark. Here are my 5 tips to help maximize your conference experience.

Develop a personal marketing plan.
You need to capitalize upon the opportunity of attending the conference. My marketing plan contained the 4 p's: product, place, price and promotion. These four constituted the marketing mix. Here is my marketing mix:
- Product: me
- Place: conference
- Price: varies depending on product or service
- Promotion: your competitive advantage

Attend the informal events.
I had the benefit of staying at the conference hotel where there were many meetups occurring. These allowed me to network with other professionals. Sometimes these meetups were more important than the sponsored events because you saw people in their raw element without pretense. These unofficial group settings made networking easier.

Practice your elevator pitch.
Your elevator pitch was indispensable towards introducing yourself. You wanted to look professional; and that means staying prepared and practicing your elevator pitch!

Have fun and explore.
Take advantage of downtime to recharge yourself. Since the conference hotel was in Times Square, I explored the area. I also traveled to Midtown and Fashion Avenue. These excursions gave me a more well-rounded experience by merging the conference with the city.

Have a post-conference action plan.
Though it was nice that you've attended the conference, created your personal media plan, practiced your elevator pitch and networked all of the events, all of those things would be for naught without implementing a post-conference action plan. Creating one is essential because once the hype and enthusiasm wore off; you don't want to be disappointed. Follow-up with thank you letters and emails mentioning the event you both attended and that you're interested in establishing a connection in the future. The recipient would remember that simple goodwill gesture.

The letter would also establish your brand as one with integrity. The post-conference action plan enabled me to never squander a conference opportunity!

Exercise: Developing your personal marketing plan

_____

_____

_____

_____

_____

_____

_____

_____

_____

_____

_____

_____

16

Developing Your Unique Selling Proposition

E VERYONE WANTS TO brush off their resumes and apply for the new jobs. The problem with this strategy is that you're doing the same thing. Last check, insanity is the doing the same thing but expecting a different result. It is my responsibility to dispense truth and not sell pipe dreams to anyone here. Therefore, I am telling you that you need to develop your unique selling proposition in order to get a new job this year.

Developing a unique selling proposition (USP) is a great way towards managing positive change. A USP is mostly associated with Fortune 500 companies, but you can still apply these tactics towards bolstering your personal career brand. Your USP lets you develop a positive career message to sell yourself in the global career marketplace.

What is a Unique Selling Proposition?
USP is what your business stands for. Businesses with a USP stand for something specific, and it becomes what you're known for.

Multinational brands like Pepsi and Cola-Cola have USPs. You must hone yours to differentiate yourself from the global competition. Yes, I mention global competition because unlike a whole lot of people on here, they are only focused on people in the United States. In the 21st century, you are competing against everyone in the world. Developing your unique selling proposition is a realistic way of landing a job. Although these are for companies, you can use USP for your personal brand.

Understanding your target audience.
When I mention your target audience, what I mean is the specific employers that fit your skill set. This is important because it is a waste of time to flood Monster and CareerBuilder with umpteen resumes with jobs that don't fit. Cultural fit is the most important part of your unique selling proposition because it doesn't matter if you get the money, if you are miserable and your coworkers are backstabbers.

What is your competitive advantage?
Your competitive advantage is the one thing distinguishing you from everyone else.

Be a Problem Solver.
Companies hire problem solvers plain and simple. Your cover letter must answer how you would solve their problems in general. In the interview, you generally solve their problems. You **DO NOT** specifically solve their problems until they hire you and start paying for your expertise.

Testing and Refining Your USP.

You have to put your USP out in the marketplace to evaluate its performance and obtain feedback. Feedback is essential towards perfecting your brand. If your USP isn't generating phone screens or interviews, then you must refine it. Non-response is feedback that you should incorporate in order to be considered.

Communicating Your USP.

In addition, you should refine your USP if you are getting interviews but no jobs. This means that you are doing something wrong in your interviews. Are you communicating that you are a problem-solver? That's one of the steps. Remember that companies hire problem solvers; therefore, if you aren't showing that you're a problem-solver, then add this into your USP.

You are a unique individual with distinguishable skills. Using these steps towards developing your unique selling proposition, increases the probability that you will land a new job.

Exercise: Finding your target audience. Use the comparative advantage feedback and build upon it.

_____

_____

_____

_____

_____

_____

_____

_____

_____

_____

_____

17

Thrive Not Strive

Strive: 1: to devote serious effort or energy: endeavor *<strive to finish a project>*

2: to struggle in opposition: contend

Thrive: *1*: to grow vigorously: flourish

2: to gain in wealth or possessions: prosper

3: to progress toward or realize a goal despite or because of circumstances —often used with *on <thrives on conflict>*

MANY PEOPLE CALL themselves strivers, but do you really want to schlep through life? Do you really want 'to continuously struggle in opposition to something'? Alternatively, do you want to 'progress towards a goal'? Thriving is much better.

Evaluate your current personal and professional routines looking for small ways to tweak them.
Examine your current personal and professional situations. Where are you? Where can you improve? Write them down then divide them into smaller parts. Find smaller ways to make a bigger

impact. One strategy is called the 1% improvement. Instead of trying to make the big leap, just make small changes to your personal and/or professional routines. These small little things can pay big dividends.

For instance, what if lunch costs $10 a day and you pack your lunch every day for one week. This small change saves you $50 this workweek. During a 4-week month, this small change will save you $200. That's a small change leading to something big. That's a great example of tweaking your daily routine in order to thrive.

See yourself as world-class.

It's hard when you're stuck in the muck and mire, trying to pay your bills. You are caught in survival mode. You just want to get through the workday, get home and take care of your children; and, then do it all over again. However, you have to view yourself as more than a widget. You're contributing something unique to the workplace. Playing to your strengths is a way to thrive in both your personal and professional lives. Read your original position description and look at why you were hired. This is one way of finding your competitive advantage. Do one thing showcasing it at work. You can do a presentation or demonstration of the new product or service. These are two ways to display your professional uniqueness. Once you own your uniqueness, you'll start seeing yourself as a world-class contributor instead of someone who fills a cubicle punching a clock! Remember, companies are resourceful. They don't waste money hiring duplicates.

The difference striving and thriving are small tweaks that will payoff huge. Commit to making these small changes so that you will have a brighter future!

Exercise: Pick out 3 areas where you can improve.

_____

_____

_____

_____

_____

_____

_____

_____

_____

_____

_____

_____

18

Personal Brand Strategy Tips

D EVELOPING A PERSONAL brand strategy is essential towards career advancement. Even before you walk into the office for an interview, your personal brand proceeds you. Here are several tips towards creating a dynamic personal brand strategy.

Your competitive advantage is your foundation.
Your competitive advantage is the one thing that you do better than anyone else. It is also the foundation towards building your personal brand strategy. You must discover it, then market it to employers to guarantee landing that job offer that you cover. The main question you must ask yourself is what sets you apart from everyone else?

Know your target market (companies that would benefit from your talents).
This is a critical step. One of the biggest mistakes that people often make is being everything to everyone. Well, you cannot do this, which is why I stress on knowing your target market. Once you've discovered your competitive advantage, research which industries are best suited for your talent. For instance, if you are a fashion

designer, you wouldn't apply for a construction job. You must know which industries complement your competitive advantage in order to successfully craft your strategy.

Know how you want to position your brand.

Brand positioning is another critical component. How are you marketing yourself? Are you entry-level, mid-level or senior-level? These are just the basics. We can drill deeper down into a category. For example, at the senior level, are you vying for a director, vice president or chairmanship position? These three different jobs require three different brand-positioning strategies. That's why you cannot be general here because you will get too many jobs that are not great fits. These generalities also waste a lot of your time sifting through these numerous positions.

Develop your pitch.

Whether you like it or not, you are always in the business of selling yourself. Developing your pitch is your way to communicate your personal brand strategy. Your pitch should be in between 15-30 seconds long and include these four factors:

- who you are,
- what you do,
- what you are looking for and,
- how you can solve a problem.

Own yourself and your content.

In the 21st century, owning your name domain is essential towards controlling your personal brand strategy; but there are so many people who don't own it. You must have your own platform to control what kind of message you want to transmit. Although social media is free, you don't want to be at the mercy of Twitter, LinkedIn or any other sites to communicate your message. Go to Name.com, Domain.com or GoDaddy.com to search your name. If it is available, then buy it. Next, buy a self-hosted WordPress site, **not anything with name.wordpress.com!** That's unprofessional but more importantly, Wordpress controls your platform. Go to WordPress.org, BlueHost or HostGator for self-hosting sites. There are many others.

I would also recommend that you start blogging on your site. Part of crafting your personal brand strategy is positioning yourself as an expert. Blogging about your professional expertise is a way to get noticed. Create content that supports your brand positioning. Write articles around your competitive advantage. The majority of my articles center around economics, brand management, change management and project management. For example, I publish my articles on my blog first before posting it on LinkedIn and Medium. There are so many people naively posting on LinkedIn who don't have their own platforms. You cannot control your message when you don't own yourself. LinkedIn owns all of your copyrights when you publish there first.

Develop a comprehensive brand marketing strategy.
In marketing, there are 4 P's: product, price, place and promotion. Here you will create a comprehensive brand marketing strategy in order to capitalize upon all available opportunities. Once you have completed all of the previous tasks, doing this is fairly easy. Here is my 4 P's:

- Product: you
- Price: current or future salary
- Place: Anywhere or your preferred region
- Promotion:

- In-person
- Online: LinkedIn, social media, blog, website, podcasting

You are the product. The price is your current or future salary. If you are going for a promotion, research salaries through sites like Glassdoor.com, so that you aren't lowballing yourself. You can also look at professional organizations because they keep salary profiles. For place, you can market yourself in a specific region or be open to relocation. Your strategy will change based on this. With promotion, you can sell yourself online as well as in-person. Always have an in-person component because you need to meet real people because it will be human resources not the computer algorithm that hires you.

Exercise: Brand positioning.
Write down which career level you are currently at (entry level, mid-level, upper level). Apply chapter 13's comparative advantage exercise as the foundation for this exercise.

_____

_____

_____

_____

_____

_____

_____

_____

_____

_____

_____

19

How to Reposition Your Brand When You Switch Careers

I N TODAY'S WORKFORCE, it is rare that you will stay in your same position your entire career. You will move into other positions and even other companies. When you do, your brand will shift along with the move. For example, you start working as a customer service representative in the call center. After 3 years, your department's manager sees that you are really good at your job, so you get promoted to customer relationship management (CRM) assistant in the market research division. Although you are in the same department (customer service), you are no longer talking with customers every day. You are now processing customers' data to generate effective marketing campaigns. There are many changes here. Not only have you been promoted, but also your new job is vastly different from your old job. Your professional brand has shifted and you need to reposition yourself for your new job. Below are my tips:

Pivot on your competitive advantage.

You must now discover what you do well on the new job. Using the CRM assistant as an example, your competitive advantage is that you can spot outliers in the data because you've spoken with the actual customers. This background knowledge helps you know that certain transactions are not in the correct group.

Over the course of my career, I have repositioned my brand five times (thus far). I have had to reposition my brand when I relocated from Cleveland to DC, promoted from Economist to Program Analyst, obtained my CAPM (Certified Associate in Project Management) license, transitioned from the public sector to private sector and, moved from employee to employer. Each time, I have to rely on a new competitive advantage to reposition my brand for greater success.

Identify what to keep, and what to let go.

Some things in your past career don't work in your current career. For instance, in the call center, your key metric is reducing churn (telephone attrition). Now that you are the CRM assistant, you are responsible for data integrity. Although keeping people on the phone and making the sales were important as a sales representative, these skills are no longer important now.

Grow your new network without alienating your current network

The important thing here is to look at the overlap. Remember, your network is your net worth. For instance, both the customer service representative and the CRM assistant work in customer service and track customers. Therefore, if the CRM data is showing irregularities, then you could still leverage your call center connections to discover why. Whenever I transition jobs or sectors, I always keep in touch with my former bosses and coworkers. You never know when you might need a favor or an unbiased professional opinion.

Exercise: Brand reevaluation – Decide what to keep and what to let go.

_____

_____

_____

_____

_____

_____

_____

_____

_____

_____

_____

_____

20

5 Steps to Brand Consistency

THERE IS TOO much poor branding out there. Every day some talking head is mentioning personal branding. No one talks about brand consistency; however, brand consistency is the way to stay memorable and relevant. Above all else, be consistent. Your effort will not matter if you aren't. Here are my 5 steps towards achieving brand consistency:

Do your research.
Doing your research is important because what you think your brand communicates isn't necessarily what the marketplace thinks. Ask people inside and outside of your company and profession, what three words come to mind whenever someone mentions you. Remember, the definition of branding is what people think of you when you are not around. If you don't conduct the appropriate market research, you will never know how consistent (or inconsistent) your brand is.

Write down your mission statement.
Your mission statement represents your current brand. To obtain a clear mission statement, ask yourself these two questions:
- What do I want my brand to accomplish?
- How do I want my brand to communicate these accomplishments?

Your mission statement must answer these questions by writing down 3 action verbs that best communicate them. This statement will serve as your brand consistency's bedrock.

Define your vision statement. This will be your tagline.
Your vision statement is your optimal future version of your brand. It can also double as your tagline. Vision statements are usually less than 20 words and they communicate your brand consistency. You will be using your mission statement as the foundation to write your vision statement.

Develop a brand communication plan.
Use your mission and vision statements to create a solid brand communication plan. It is essential to control how your brand is transmitted. Although you work in a company, your brand must consistently communicate wherever you go. This is why I have broken down 4 audiences that will receive your brand message.

Below is a graph showing 4 quadrants. The columns represent organizational structure. They are departments (internal) and professional network (external). The rows represent people. They are coworkers, industry professionals (internal), company employees, and regular workers (external).

	Department (Internal)	Network (External)
People (Internal)	Coworkers	Workers in your profession but outside the company
People (External)	Employees out-side your dept.	Workers outside both your profession and company

The first quadrant represents your coworkers, both inside your immediate department and whom you interact with on a daily basis. They are the ones whom you communicate the most. The second quadrant represents the company employees' who work in the same building but not the same department. Although they have the same company structure, their departmental culture may differ from yours. The third quadrant represents the work-ers in your professional network whom share your occupation but not your company. Your commonality is your industry but they work in different company cultures. The fourth quadrant represents the people whom are both outside your company and profession. When writing your brand communication plan, **write for the people in this fourth quadrant.** These people are unfamiliar with your industry jargon and company culture. If they understand your brand and what it represents, then you have achieved brand consistency.

Execute your plan and collect feedback.

Once you have created your plan, start implementing it. Roll it out to all four quadrants and await feedback. Collecting feedback is critical towards evaluating your brand's consistency level. If your industry or company has changed, these changes would be recorded in your feedback. Incorporate it back into your brand to achieve brand consistency for the long-term.

Using these 5 tips would help you achieve brand consistency.

Exercise: Write brand communication plan. You can use the communication plan's exercise as an input if you want.

_____

_____

_____

_____

_____

_____

_____

_____

_____

_____

_____

_____

Bibliography

Chapter 3: Employing the Three Cs (Clarity, Consistency, Constancy) to Improve Your Personal Career Brand
Personal Branding for Dummies, Susan Chritton, Second Edition, 2012, Wiley Business Books. New York, New York.

Chapter 4: Handling High-Visibility Projects As a Newbie
http://smallbusiness.chron.com/strategic-project-10440.html

Chapter 8: 5 Differences between busy and productive people
Fast Company: The Three Biggest Differences Being Busy and Being Productive
http://www.fastcompany.com/3051920/secrets-of-the-most-productive-people/the-three-biggest-differences-being-busy-and-productiv

Entrepreneur: 3 Steps to Stop Being Busy and Start Being Productive
https://www.entrepreneur.com/article/229625

Chapter 11: Avoiding Scope Creep
Project Management Body of Knowledge (PMBOK)
- Crashing definition. Page 535. 2013. Project Management Institute. Newton Square, PA.
- scope definition. Page 562. 2013. Project Management Institute. Newton Square, PA.

Chapter 16: Unique Selling Proposition
Kissmetrics: Unique Selling Proposition
https://blog.kissmetrics.com/unique-selling-proposition/

Marketing Donut: Developing Your Unique Selling Proposition: A Step-by-Step Guide
http://www.marketingdonut.co.uk/marketing/marketing-strategy/branding/developing-your-usp-a-step-by-step-guide

Thank You

I would like to thank the following people for this book. Your guidance and encouragement could not be underestimated. My family, Suet Bourdhaa, Sharvette Mitchell, Melanie Bonita, Robin E Devonish, La Tanyha Boyd and Rock Your Book, Danyelle Little, Yolanda Spinks, Think Positive Radio and Magazine, Tiana von Johnson, Francina Harrison, Adrienne Graham, Jai Stone, Chaz Kyser, Anita Jacobs, Desiree Lee, Arvin Poole, Pollie Massey and Cove. You have helped me throughout this journey and I am grateful for your reassurance and wisdom.

www.ingramcontent.com/pod-product-compliance
Lightning Source LLC
Chambersburg PA
CBHW020844210326
41598CB00019B/1967